My Journal

Made in the USA
Coppell, TX
02 May 2021

54831554R00069